play

D1475937

work

lose

win

wet

down

false

true

bottom

top

messy

tidy

thin

thick

wild

tame

short

sunset

sunrise

friend

stranger

stop

leave

stay

earn

spend

sour

sweet

sharp

receive

send

different

same

wrong

right

poor

rich

lower

raise

start

quit

slow

quick

pull

push

ugly

pretty

fancy

plain

fail

pass

whole

part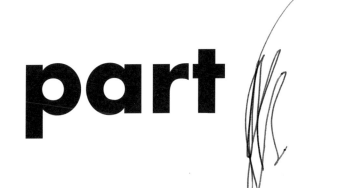

under

over

close

open

on

young

old

far

near

loud

hate

love

lost

tight

loose

short

long

dark

light

more

less

right

left

follow

lead

cry

laugh

small

large

sadness

cruel

kind

outside

inside

cold

hot

soft

hard

bad

good

funny

back

front

enemy

friend

last

first

slow

fast

fiction

fact

odd

even

empty

hard

easy

earth

shallow

deep

night

day

come

dirty

clean

sell

buy

fix

break

afraid

white

black 9

big

ending

beginning

before

asleep

awake

together

apart

subtract

add

below

above

78 common opposite word pairs are included in *Flip-Flash™ Phonics: Opposites*.

above	white	earth	enemy	kind	dark	old	ugly	send	sunset	wet
below	brave	sky	front	cruel	long	young	push	receive	tall	dry
add	afraid	easy	back	joy	short	on	pull	sharp	short	win
subtract	break	hard	funny	sadness	loose	off	quick	dull	tame	lose
apart	fix	empty	sad	large	tight	open	slow	sweet	wild	work
together	buy	full	good	small	lost	close	quit	sour	thick	play
awake	sell	even	bad	laugh	found	over	start	spend	thin	
asleep	clean	odd	hard	cry	love	under	raise	earn	tidy	
before	dirty	fact	soft	lead	hate	part	lower	stay	messy	
after	come	fiction	high	follow	loud	whole	rich	leave	top	
beginning	go	fast	low	left	quiet	pass	poor	stop	bottom	
ending	day	slow	hot	right	many	fail	right	go	true	
big	night	first	cold	less	few	plain	wrong	stranger	false	
little	deep	last	inside	more	near	fancy	same	friend	up	
black	shallow	friend	outside	light	far	pretty	different	sunrise	down	

Why Learn About Opposites?

Knowing opposites will:
- increase vocabulary
- improve reading comprehension
- improve writing skills and
- increase performance on standardized tests!

Helpful Hints for Learning Opposites

Flip and Check   An *antonym* is a word having the *opposite* meaning of another word.

Read the word on one side. Think of a word with the opposite meaning. Say the opposite. Flip the page to check.

Extensions
Look for more opposite word pairs to add to the words in this book.

Find words that have the *same* meaning as the words in this book. Those words are *synonyms*, words with the same or nearly the same meaning.

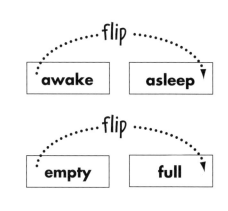

Mc Graw Hill McGraw-Hill Children's Publishing

Published by Ideal School Supply
An imprint of McGraw-Hill Children's Publishing
Copyright © 2002 McGraw-Hill Children's Publishing

All Rights Reserved • Printed in Malaysia

No part of this publication may be reproduced, stored in a retrieval system, or transmitted, in any form or by any means, electronic, mechanical, photocopying, recording, or otherwise, without the prior written permission of the publisher.

ISBN 156451394-7

Send all inquiries to:
McGraw-Hill Children's Publishing
3195 Wilson Drive NW
Grand Rapids, Michigan 49544

Flip-Flash™ Phonics: Opposites

2 3 4 5 6 7 8 9 TWP 07 06 05 04 03 02

9 781564 513946

The **McGraw-Hill** Companies